Storm Warning

The New Canadian Poets

D0291398

Storm Warning

The New Canadian Poets

Edited by Al Purdy

McClelland and Stewart Limited

Toronto/Montreal

0-7710-7191-4

This book was designed by David Shaw

The Canadian Publishers
McClelland and Stewart Limited
25 Hollinger Road, Toronto 374

Printed in Canada

Storm Warning

Photographs and statements of some of the poets
were not available.

Kerrigan Almey

Ken Belford

Runs a trapline and homesteads
near South Hazelton, B.C.
Is rumor and legend, hence may
not have been born in 1946
as has been bruited about. Book,
Fireweed (Talonbooks).

Born 1948, Trenton, Ont.
"Been had by as many different
jobs as all the other liars."
Books, *A Handbook For Comrades* ("Regrettable!") and
For All The Squares (forthcoming).

bill bissett

Gregory Cook

Born in 1942, Yarmouth, N.S.
Progressed "from farm to
university by baptizing, marry-
ing and burying as Baptist
preacher." Married and un-
buried himself. Immersed
in several mags. Teaches.

Born 1939, Nova Scotia. Most
experimental of all Canadian
poets (some say). Has published
some dozen books with Blew
Ointment Press and others.
Doubtful if he knows how many
books he's written. Several
Canada Council Awards. Does
not teach.

Louis Cormier

Terry Crawford

Born 1948, New Brunswick.
Book, *The Silent Cowboys of the
East* (Fiddlehead). Won
Bliss Carman Poetry Award at
U.N.B. two successive years.
Edits Intercourse. Has spoken
to Allen Ginsberg.

Born 1945, St. John, N.B.
Poems in several little mags.
Book, *Lost Neighbourhood*
(Fiddlehead). Married. Works.

Phil DesJardins　　　　　　**Deborah Eibel**

Born 1947, Quebec. "Married,
teacher, editor." Book, *The
Starlings Didn't* (forthcoming).

Born 1940, Montreal, Que.
Educated at McGill and Rad-
cliffe. Canada Council
Award, 1967-68. Poems in many
little and big mags. Teaches.

Doug Fetherling

Brenda Fleet

Born 1948, Quebec City. French
mother and English-speaking
father. B.A. from Bishop's Univ.
Book, *Catching the Sun's Fire*
(Fiddlehead). Writing a novel.
Lives in North Hatley, Que.
Married.

Quebec   55
To Mother, on a Winter
    Day   59
*Statement   60

Says of himself: "please re-
member that I was not born any-
where nor at any time
(except maybe the late 1940's)."
Books, *The United States of
Heaven* (Anansi), and *Our Man
In Utopia* (forthcoming).
Lives in utopian Toronto.

Your Absence Has not Taught
    Me   52
A London Hermit Looks on the
    Bright Side   52
*Statement   54

Gail Fox   **Dana Fraser**

Born 1942, Willimantic, Conn.,
U.S. Books, *Dangerous
Season* (Quarry Press) and *The
Royal Collector of Dreams*
(Fiddlehead). Has lived in Can-
ada since 1964. Married. One
child: Jason.

Born 1944, Vancouver, B.C.
Published in several
magazines. "I write poems for
personal credibility," she
says. Is "a women's lib fanatic."
Married. Works.

Gary Geddes   **C. H. Gervais**

Is spending a year in England.
Edited *20th Century Poetry
and Poetics* for Oxford Uni-
versity Press and is a co-editor
of Copp Clark's *Studies in
Canadian Literature* series.

Born, 1946, in Ontario. "At 14
I wrote a 190 page book on
how Canada could strategically
take over the *Panhandle* from
the Americans. At 17 began writ-
ing poetry." Book, *A Sym-
pathy Orchestra* (forthcoming).
Edits *Black Moss*. Lives in
Fergus, Ontario.

Howard Halpern

David Helwig

Born 1949, Toronto, Ont.
Became U.S. citizen in 1963.
Returns to Canada four
years later, renouncing U.S.
citizenship. 1970, barred
entry to U.S. Poetry in several
magazines.

BUMP   70
*Statement   72

Born 1938, Toronto, Ont.
Youth in Niagara, old age in
Kingston. Books, *Figures
in a Landscape, The Streets of
Summer* and *The Sign of
the Gunman* (all Oberon Press).
Is the best-known poet included
here.

Bill Howell

Patrick Lane

Born 1939, Nelson, B.C. Veteran
young poet. "Lived always in
interior mountain country"
where it's picturesque and scenic,
until he got mixed up with
shady characters in publishing
and writing. Several books.
Lives in B.C.

Born 1946, Halifax, N.S.
Torontonian from the Mari-
times, or vice-versa. Works
for C.B.C. Archives. Novel and
book of poems scheduled for
publication. Unmarried.

Dennis Lee

Bernell Macdonald

Born 1948, O'Leary, P.E.I.
(how about that?) Fourth year
arts student at U.N.B.,
Fredricton. Book, *I Can Really
Draw Eagles* (Fiddlehead).

it is you that makes the song   97

Born 1939, Toronto, Ont.
(Very WASPish!) Three books,
of which *Civil Elegies* is the
best. Directs House of Anansi
Press. Lives in Toronto.
Married. Some cats.

1883   90
Third Elegy   91
Thursday   94
More Claiming   95
*Statement   96

David McFadden

Barry McKinnon

Born 1940, Hamilton, Ontario.
Proof reads for Hamilton
Spectator. Published several
books, and in many mags.
Prolific. Married. Children. His
collected works in 1999 will
contain 10,000 poems.

Born 1944, Calgary, Alta.
Member of Irving Layton's
poetry class in Montreal,
1965-67. Denies Leonard Cohen
influence. Book, *The Golden
Daybreak Hair* (Aliquondo
Press). Forthcoming, *The Car-
casses of Spring*. Married.
Teaches.

Tom Marshall

Sid Marty

Born 1938, Niagara Falls, Ont.
Has written a book on D.H.
Lawrence and edited one on
A.M. Klein. Poetry, *The
Silences of Fire* (Macmillan).
Editor of Quarry Press. Teaches.

Born 1944, in England. Father,
Canadian soldier. Lived in
Alberta from age 2. Has B.A.
In summer, works as Park
Warden in Jasper and Yoho
National Parks. Published
in several little mags. Married.
Two dogs.

David Phillips

Marc Plourde

Born 1951, Montreal, Que. One
book with Fiddlehead Poetry
Books. Fr.-Can. and English-
Can. parents.

Born 1944, Vancouver, B.C.
Four years at U.B.C. Has lived
in bush cabin in northern
Ont., and worked in apple and
cherry orchards. Now in
North Van. Books, *The Dream
Outside* (Coach House) and
Wave (Talonbooks).

Andrew Suknaski

Tom Wayman

Born 1942, Wood Mountain,
Sask. Jobs: grocer, fence-builder,
farm laborer, bull cook,
night watchman, bellman (what's
that?), window washer, stone-
picker, etc. Also, potter, litho-
grapher, sculptor, etc. Writes
poems too.

Born 1945, Hawkesbury, Ont.
U.B.C. grad. Instructor in
English and writing at Colorado
State Univ., 1968-69. Mem-
ber: *Students for Democratic
Society*, 1966-69. Member of
I.W.W. (Wobblies, to you.)
Now a laborer. Was a boy scout.

Ian Young

Dale Zieroth

Born 1946, Neepawa, Man.
Left university at 18, Jobs:
teacher, laborer, book shipper,
now archivist at C.B.C.
Married and lives in Toronto.
Two cats.

Born 1945, London (England,
that is). Writes, edits and
translates in Scarborough, Ont.
Book, *Year of the Quiet Sun*
(Anansi).

For John Newlove,
who has worked almost as hard
on this book as myself –
and whom I can blame or praise,
depending on who attacks me
as an editor.   AWP.

Acknowledgements

To the individual poets, some of whose poems have appeared in *Sunday Work, Made in Canada, Fiddlehead, either/or, Performing Arts in Canada, Canadian Forum, West Coast Seen, Fifteen Winds* and *Vigilante*.

Ken Belford's poems appeared in his Talonbook, *Fireweed*; bill bissett's *poem* is from his book, *The Lost Angel Mining Company* (blewointment press); Gail Fox's poems appeared in her *The Royal Collector of Dreams* (Fiddlehead Books); Patrick Lane's *Wild Horses* and *Ten Miles in from Horsefly* appeared in *Separations* (New/Books); Dennis Lee's *Third Elegy* is taken from his *Civil Elegies* (House of Anansi); David Helwig's *A Footnote to the Election* was taken from his book *The Sign of the Gunman* and is reprinted by permission of Oberon Press.

Introduction

In earlier anthologies of young Canadian poets editors have claimed a great deal of merit – not to say roaring genius – for their own chosen stable of poets. So I'd like to strike a modest sort of claim myself. I believe several of the poets in this book will supplant (tho not necessarily eclipse) the present-day literary establishment in Canada.

This is surely a modest claim: that such writers as Sid Marty, Tom Wayman, David McFadden, Dennis Lee, Bill Howell, Andrew Suknaski, Dale Zieroth and others will replace the Birneys and Laytons and Cohens in the near future. And a good thing too. A good thing that the roots keep growing, even tho their own roots are the writers they replace.

Two poets in this collection have already made their talents very evident: David Helwig and Tom Marshall. Perhaps also David McFadden – altho up to now McFadden's public circulation has been small and in-groupish.

But even in making such a modest claim for some of the poets I've chosen, there is strong possibility of error on my part. Someone whose name does not occur to me here may get his/her second wind and overtake all the others in the race. For it is a race – against themselves and time. The time they think they have, and the time there really is. A race against themselves, because all races are against our own limitations. In dramatic terms: to flare briefly, and drive for the finish line like sweating runners; body and brain united, briefly at their best, to produce, merely – a few good poems.

Some might think that a small reward for the lifetime's effort necessary. I think it is a great reward. For there is no one thing in the world I think more worthwhile than writing good poems – which encompasses and includes all the other activities of life.

For purposes of this collection, an upper age limit was imposed on possible contributors. I'm not altogether happy with that arbitrary cut-off point, but I agree with Jack McClelland and the McStew editors that it's necessary to proclaim some kind of boundaries – whether geographic or chronological. Nevertheless, I regret the absence here of Margaret Simard and Des Loan particularly. They are unknowns who wrote good poems; but their comparative senility (37 and 40) precluded inclusion.

Also arbitrary is the choice of poets themselves and their specific poems presented here. That choice was mine, and has to consist of my personal belief that certain poems and poets are good. No doubt poets were omitted (other than the two named above) who will prove in future what my near-sighted eyes and brain were not able to see: that they were/are better than I thought they were/are.

But again, that's my responsibility. And going even farther, my choice was made on the basis of good poems rather than poets, which may seem a minute distinction. In that connection, John Newlove, now a McStew editor, said to me challeng-ingly: "Not enough western poets!" So we counted them up together, and decided that the regional representation was actually fair and adequate (Didn't we, John?).

To stress this point: I haven't included anyone in this book because he/she was a rising young poet or represented a special geo-graphic area. That's idealistic possibly (in view of regional sales), and proclaiming my honesty in this way is taking credit for what was actually more or less accidental.

And now, in spite of feeling that editing a book like this one is "a reward in itself," I'm sick of reading so many poems. By which I mean good, bad or indifferent poems. I'm soaked, saturated, immersed and marinated in poems. (I don't want to see another lousy poem until at least tomorrow!)

In the final month of editing this book, I haven't written any poems myself: sterility I wouldn't have believed possible in myself. As a result of such personal barrenness, I'm tempted to say to the possible reader: if you don't like the book to hell with you. But I can't say that. Despite being sick of writing many letters and reading many poems, I think the result of all that work is a good book and that these are good poems. For they reveal what we are thinking and feeling as human beings, not so different now than it ever was or even will be – here in Canada and in the world. Explicitly and implicitly thru them all, runs the flare of being alive. Dylan Thomas said it too, thru the mouth of Polly Garter: "Isn't life a terrible thing – thank God!"

Al Purdy

Kerrigan Almey

Someday Jason

You will be twenty
one and I am
and I am basically a loser
but right now Jason sweet
child inspiration for your
mother's poetry and life and love
right now Jason I am
a winner
Jason I see your mother
as she is and you can
not and Jason
you lose.

Kerrigan Almey

*Statement

".....Won't say much about spring and love, other than I'm kinda happy sometimes, learning about wiping kids' asses, and even making out a little bit. Writing some, but the same old deal – nothing really spontaneously beautiful – manufacturing poems and out of five, maybe one....."

".....I'd like to be editor of the thing, but I'm not an academic; get all my educating from day to day, so will have to start my own church sometime....."

".....I should like the opportunity to verify and versify the what and why of myself, since little is accomplished here in ambiguity and brevity, but to continue thus would betray my trade and I have promises to keep and poetry to write, and the liquor store is quite a brisk shuffle down the street and I must toddy on....."

Ken Belford

Omega

The dog in the snowbank is dead
Because he trusted me as meat
And I fed him wine for a laugh.

That even with innocence I cannot be trusted
Is one more reason why
There is nothing to laugh about.

The first was to make my own law.
The second was to break it. To distinguish the limits.
Apparently, the third is to pay for it.

To repay, purify, you heap one death onto another.
You trade a twenty-five dollar wolf hide for the dog,
Figuring somehow that one more death equals zero.

You are not expected
To know
What it is like.

But I hunted all day on the surrealistic ice.
Until I stood there in the belly of night,
Listening. . . .

To the circling sound of furred feet
Pacing the edge of my flashlight limit.
And I just stood there wondering if it was a wolf or a dog.

It is the same problem here.
The alternative is to believe.
Bitter

Aloe, how cleansing
From the flower gun aimed in the darkness.
And there is nothing to laugh into.

Ken Belford

Still Shots Echo

Still shots echo in a deliberate land,
Almost daring me
To go too far into it.

I've squinted down gun barrels here,
And closed the other eye
When I squeezed the trigger.

There's an abnormal fusion at the other ends of my sight.
And the poles I've believed in 'till now
Come turning back upon themselves.

But I hunt the Arctic grouse.
Tho always I know that to another kind of eye,
There might be nothing here.

A small grey circle of smoke drifts away from me.
A cigarette drops at my feet.
Cold fingertips meet melt and stick to colder steel.

Hit. The startled bird lifts its already dying body
And clumsily drifts across the river
To die on the other side. No one can cross here.

There is no prize today.
And a deeper silence. No echo now.
And I wonder if a law has been broken,

Feeling that I've shot more than a bird
Hung out there
At the end of a dry limb.

Ken Belford

Odd Horses

Me and the odd horses
By the edge
Of something.

Donna, she rides them,
And thinks if she can't get near
A new horse there is something wrong with it.

Does she
Know those odd horses are just
Like my friends?

Ken Belford

Erasure

i

It is hard to tell how far away
The mountains really are. They seem closer,
But they must be fifteen miles, maybe more.

And what is between is like an August haze.
Only it is not. It is February and cold.
My eyes travelling to that edge again.

To what is a thickening mist.
Both sheltering and raging
Against what I can half see.

ii

I know how thin the crust is in parts.
I know that mist as fear. Behind it is the avalanche.
My poems are small cries: nothing more.

Ken Belford

*Statement

Poetry for me is like a keyhole, something I can drain myself
through, really another world on the other side of the door.

I believe I have eaten winter at Takla Landing . . . a dog in that
country is a buck . . . pumping his heart. . . I had to shoot
three horses . . . something that I had to face . . . everything seemed
to go wrong . . . the lantern fell apart . . . all I had left was a
flashlight – that's when I started to write the good poetry.

bill bissett

th average canadian nose bleed

Sunday morning in Oakalla
pickin' off the crabs, tryin'
to break their backs, or

failin' that, drown 'em
in th overflowd sink, at
least can keep their numbers

down, rumor has it theres to be
a street movie shown today;
last nite on tv – burt lancaster

katherine hepburn in Th Rainmaker,
such a beautiful film, th message,
yu are what yu see yrself

to be, th ultimate in sentimental
solipsism, democracy, th faith
of our times, even J. Paul Getty

wud agree, etc., but hepburn
shows th truth of it, wud she becum
wholly human, that is, make it

with illusion, th camp of mid-west
pioneer nostalgia, etc., only th deluge
Starbuck promises cud possibly know

as th 10 pm curfew struck long befor
this really great etc. movie was ovr
nd the guards regretfully themselves

had to turn off th set, while th rest
of us were lockd in this lonely instance,
like, how do you spell realize

oakalla prison farm
jan/69

33

bill bissett

mother earth

both th prosecutor at th last sentencing nd
Louis Dudek at the Poets Conference in T.O.
sd if he's any good as a poet he'll write just

as well inside jail as on th street:
i think this is a lousy pome
what do yu think, shit-head reader.

where do yu think yu are, heaven (already)

oakalla prison farm
jan/69

poem

   Her blondebeauty subduing th warring demons, her
dark beauty subduing th warring demons, her brown
beauty subduing th warring demons, her yellow
beauty subduing th warring demons, her black
beauty subduing th warring demons, her red beauty
subduing th warring demons, of power: this is
the gold of which we all speak, and this is what
th guns mean.

bill bissett

anothur 100 warrants issued

*(newsflash: 7 men entered a Vancouver graveyard
only to disappear in a flash of white light*

Whats it like o straight person
square john to be abul to shop
around say at th 3 Vets or th
Army & Navy without being stopped
harassed etc. by th Narks at every turn
yu take, hey, whats it like
to get up in th morning, gatherd,
yu nd yr friends close ones, around
th warming stove without the R.C.M.P.
crashing thru th veils within th
bardo of mistrust, Canada, etc.,
how duz it feel, yr children,
terrorized, hiding, facing jail
or what is sumtimes worse, parole,
to have a Nark recognize yu so
that there is no recourse, markd
yu advocate nothing except
humanity and only th overthrow
of this state's tryranny, yu go thru
th streets on fire as an alarm
to yr friends as they get nabbd
this week of Jan 7/69 in Vancouver,
the Narks go thru th houses, ripping
apart floor boards, cupboards, children's
dolls, in a red convertible, Caesar's
computer men, bullet heads, pigs,
whats it like o yu who feel yu are
citizens of this sold-out Grandmother's
land to not have pigs vomitting at yu
all th time, to stand trial for
ovr a year, to see friends jailed
for 3 years for keeping th peace
with themselves their world etc.

35

bill bissett

*Statement

i gess yu cud tell th soul what is it hungrs too maybe i cin lern
to sew take up leathr work but it too wud take yeers of hard
mean it work total miss undrstanding anxious divinities long hours
mistr boss is evryehr no one i know gud gets paid very much
fr poetry neithr nd fr th care of language sum care with each othr
sailin thru th fleshy bardos th cracked ice aint too thin wintr moon
write in send $ yu dont need to spell or follow any rules lettrs from
th sand bfor yr mind yr fingrs turn to dust yr warlords sell yu
trade yu fr steel toes nylon eyes tendr missiles dance baby up from
th concrete thers straw all ovr th official documents head-
quarters is floodid. . . .

Gregory Cook

Poet Parodies Professor/Lover's Quarrel

(To Alden Nowlan)

Suddenly, you've not only drawn the battlelines,
     it's as though your seeing him will make him so.
He retaliates, and will fight to the finish,
     which is the last thing he wants, but it's easier,
always easier to fight than become what he must.

Gregory Cook

*Statement

This is to certify that our right trusty and well-beloved GREGORY
COOK having by his wisdom and many and varied intellectual
and humane accomplishments proved himself worthy of our affec-
tion, admiration and trust, has been elevated by us to the rank
of KNIGHT COMMANDER in our Most Noble and Beneficient
Order of the Golden Phallus of St. George of Cappadoccia,
and LORD CHANCELOR of our Wolfville, N.S., Chapter of
our Society of St. Simeon the Mad, which rank and appointment
further entitle him to the honour of REAR ADMIRAL in our
Fleet, Given under our hand and seal, in this year of our Lord, one
thousand and seventy, and in the thirty-seventh year of the
Salusian Era,

Alden P.
Alden, Prince of Fortara, Count of the Holy Roman Empire,
Crown Bearer to the Kings of Leinster

Louis Cormier

Testament

The sandals move softly
over images of water,
the soft, brown sandals
carrying him over the heads
of his apostles
in King Square,
Saint John,
as he, the great Messiah
of the clouded Word
brings incense messages
from his Gethsemane,
venturing forth
to preach the gospel
according to Pot,
chapter twelve,
verse three:
"Fellow hippies,
skin, and greasers,
tragic news from
the fuzz-house,
John and David
hath been busted."
A cataclysmic hush
descends over the flowers
as two lovers fall upon the grass
and loyal followers
retire to Pete's place
for the wine.

Louis Cormier

The Stubborn Fella, Leaving Home

I told the dogs
on Victoria Street
I'd bring 'em all back
a bone,
with some meat
left on it,
from wherever
I was going.
I told the telephone poles
they had carried
too many wrong numbers
and that I'd get 'em for it
sooner or later.
I told the Baptist church
across the street
it needed some color
in its Sunday sermons.
At the doorway,
I looked back up the stairs
through the dirty
door windows,
tried to close
the door with no handle
as tight as I could.
"Leavin' home are yuh?"
said the sidewalk boys.
"Yup."
"There'll be more
wrong numbers,
stupid,"
said the telephone wires.
"Go dial a dog bone,"
I yelled,
and left triumphant
to the yapping of dogs.

Louis Cormier

*Statement

No one's come back from the lake yet to go up the hill to play
ball.

Up the street I look and sure enough it's my father with his lunch
can coming home early from work, accident, he's limping, not
saying a word. Not saying a word I watch him come up to our front
door and look across the street at me and not smile and open
the door and go upstairs and the door rocks back and forth a few
times after he's gone. I cross over to our doorway on the shaded
side of the street to listen for voices upstairs, to find out what
happened. Careless man on the girder, foolish foolish man, didn't
have enough sense to yell. Crushed foot, doctor says he can
still work in a week or two, though, if he's careful. That's good.
Relieved. Walk back out into the street feeling confused, no one's
back from the lake.

Saint John, 1962/Montreal, 1970 .

Terry Crawford

Thaw (for Donna)

Hearing you softly crying
and sensing your slightly
sullen disappointment
over the long distance line
I ventured out in sub-zero
January and begged
a truck driver
who didn't trust my looks
enough to let me ride in the cab
to at least carry me
in the open box
and was gratified to hear
the driver say to his helper
(28 miles from Saint John
shouting over a country & western radio)
"Well, he's tougher than he looks,
he's still with us."
But the cold, the cold,
I couldn't have been in the truck,
I was somewhere out front
suspended in a silver tunnel
the headlights were thrusting
through the monotonous darkness
of the New Brunswick night;
I might as well have been
a minute Jonah in a salmons belly
being carried under the ice
all the way to Fredericton.

Oh, how I cursed you for your loneliness
and called myself stupid
for falling toward your distant tears,
I cursed the black woods away,
cursed away the powder snow
wisping past the tail gate,
cursed away the miles . . .
"Alright mack time to get out."
How did I walk the last five blocks?
My feet felt like my legs
were cut off at the knees,
my hands (being curled fists
inside my dandified dress gloves)
couldn't open the back door
so that I elbowed the window
or perhaps even banged it with my head
till you awoke and came
looking so warmly sleepy
and mildly awed and amazed
that I laughed at your silliness
as we got into bed
and I thawed inside your embrace
and again laughed at myself
for loving you so much.

Terry Crawford

The Heat's On

In the heat of sleep
we may dream . . .
someone elses terror.
Last night I saw a smiling,
laughing Christ who loved simp-
ly because he felt love.
In the dream
I came to know
that Jesus knew an un-
earthly terror
     when he could feel
  himself ascending
into the high dry air
and could hear
     angels
whispering in his ear.

  O, how he struggled to re-
    Gain the Earth!

He never expected
    to have to believe
  in himself.

Terry Crawford

*Statement

My poems are an attempt to discover the various kinds of magic
people believe in along with the devils that haunt them. I
guess we're all pretty ridiculous, fools really, but we have our
moments of brilliance when we see how the magic works,
perceive small miracles or exorcize a devil. We're all poor in
some way too, each of us reaching for different riches.
The nuns who taught me were fond of saying, "If you're poor,
God has a special place for you." On the diamond, playing
baseball (the most mystic of games) we used to reply, "Yeah . . .
Hell." With a laugh of course. It was small magic but did have
miraculous power.

Phil DesJardins

Tonight It Isn't Simple Things

in the past
toothaches have cracked the drawl
spilled the content of night
    things simple as toothaches
    or gushing dreams
ran a fine clean finger line
down the soaped glass
preview of renovated selves   tonight
it isn't simple things
that weigh the drawbridge open
and keep the water sounding up between
tight board dreams that rain on after catharsis
it's the images of scorched children
flaked like the crust on apple pie
and the sonic gurgle
    of dishwater piped down from a sink
    one late floor up
of the annoyance at finding a spoon

Phil DesJardins

Trapper

I'm thinking how the cabin was
the wicker chair
still soft for dozing
before the logs I left full
fired to keep the room
and bed warm as a woman.
I set my boots to dry
a cup of hot rum
and sorted the traps for one more line trip
three silver fox would bring
enough for new sled
runners and good strong harnesses
for the team.
God   the wind cuts deep tonight but
it pushes me on
across the frozen lake.

Phil DesJardins

*Statement

As a teacher, I am daily compelled to see life through the eyes
of children. It is less conscious compulsion than something
I do naturally. I have never lost this sense of wonder. Ordinary
adults lose that aura at several points in the deliberate act of
growing up.

Much of my poetry rattles with this concern for very simple things
– often it can be imagined as being seen through the eyes of a
child – at least the metaphors play on that expansive ground.

There is, of course, the reverse of this childlike domain and it can
give rise to poetry of protest – of a kind. The protest against
the sacrifice of childlike qualities for the "maturity" of adulthood.
Education is at fault here, and science.

Deborah Eibel

The Man Who Married Colvin Kell

After a spinsterhood of many years,
Colvin Kell, the illiterate charwoman
Who spoke in the dictum
Of those initiated by the wind,
Who never worried about decorum,
Accepted the offer of an unlikely man,
One who had been rejected by other charwomen,
Because he was shiftless.
But Colvin Kell, being a grammarian among charwomen,
Could read his mind.
Because she used the wind as "vade-mecum," as gloss,
He was never too inscrutable for her.
She accepted him, because he was a whole man:
He loved caterpillar and moth and butterfly,
Wood and fire and ash.

Late marriage was meaningful
In ways that earlier marriage could not have been.
The pastimes that mattered now
Could not have mattered before.
Nothing could have mattered before.
They loved to walk in stony places:
They verified themselves by kicking stones.
They honoured each other.
She kept the floors and walls and woodwork
Immaculate for him.
Delighted with her art,
He scratched "Colvin fecit"
On whatever she touched.
(These are the only words she ever learned to read.)
He paid further tribute
By playing his flute.
When she asked him
Why he repeated the melody hour after hour
Without embellishing it,
He said that for this theme
There could be no variations.

But one day, years later,
When he thought her back was turned,
He changed.
She understood what was happening.
She had known from the first
That a change must come about, sooner or later,
That he would one day lean away, break away.
(After all, had he not married beneath his station?)
That day, he did not ask her to go walking with him,
But she left the kitchen anyway and followed at a distance.
There were stones on the road;
He walked around them instead of kicking them.

He embellished the flute melody,
For which, he had said before,
There could be no variations.

It was dark, it was raining, he was old.
He agreed to come home.
He went to sleep.
Colvin Kell knew that he was searching
For a carnival place, for hilarity.
They would not meet again, anywhere.
(She did not mean that he was necessarily lost,
For he had not been a worthless man.
But there would always be distance between them.)

Just before he left,
All seasons converged on his tongue.
After his departure, they realigned themselves.

Deborah Eibel

*Statement

The poems that seem important to me are those that reflect my
passion for music. They concern listeners, listening habits.
If I were to write an autobiography, I would probably begin by
explicating such poems of mine as Death of a Goldfish, The
Wife of Rabbi Israel ben Eliezer, Scene of King Harold's Death
Revisited, My Father Was a Prophet, Children of the Ghetto
Dream of Tel-Aviv, A New Era, and Of Spinsters.

Doug Fetherling

Your Absence Has not Taught Me.

Your absence has not taught me
how to be alone, it merely has
shown that when together we cast
a single shadow upon this wall.
The wall I suppose is as a wall
should be: plain and bare and
final as a cliff. And when I
stretch, my hand finds it instead
of you and I invent truths men
thought of years ago without
telling me.

VI.70.

A London Hermit Looks on the Bright Side

I have no telephone
I have no timepiece
I have no radio
I have no telly
And I do not read the papers for I have
no interest in rape
I learn about the weather when it happens
I go to the cinema rarely and only stay
for the adverts
But I sometimes take walks in the courtyard
or, less often, take out the rubbish

My sole contact with the world then
is the electricity meter I have come to adore
Jutting like an ear from the wall
where it's screwed, it breaks up the pattern
of all those fleurs-de-lys
With the unfaltering regularity
of Almighty unfaltering God, it clicks
off the kilowatt hours between one week
and another

It now reads oh-oh-sixty-nine
The postman came but left me nothing
at oh-oh-sixty-six and I have not bathed
or eaten since oh-oh-sixty-four
Minus five-five-seventeen was the year
the first Kennedy was shot
And though Rome fell before electricity
was known my newfound system can easily
pinpoint this or any reality at will

My bathtub has a ring indelible under torture
My ashtrays are like massacre sites high up
in the Andes
The gas is not connected so my stove sits
in its crate
and my frig, unpacked but plugless,
serves better as a bookcase
Being as I am a batchelor I lack
a certain fulfilment in life
which my meter has supplied me
these long months under lamplight

Doug Fetherling

*Statement

To me, the purest form of writing is good journalism. Not the
daily press poppycock but the type every new generation for the
past three or four has called or thought of as the New
Journalism: free, not uncolourful reportage whose sole aim is
truth in all fields at any cost. The best poetry, like the best
fiction or the best advertising, is essentially this kind of writing
except that it is internal rather than external. Lately I have
been doing a lot of love poems, but in these too (or at least in the
best ones, I hope) I have reported with some accuracy what
happens emotionally in certain situations.

Brenda Fleet

Quebec

I.

My city, my old terraces,
With the few cobble roads that remain,
The men that work and sweat at your ferry,
Why have you remained so inarticulate
Why so impassive? The clash of traffic
Defiles you; you have forgotten your past;
And still you turn to me
For a song of faithfulness.

Take a good look at yourself first!
What do you know of the rest of the world?
Your naiveté astounds me!
History has rushed past you,
And you toy with your blank thoughts
As if you were toothless and senile
Taking your pleasure from the fraying
Churches and towers that are left
Smiling at the riverbank, decaying . . .

A slave who knows nothing
A slave without pride
Offering little resistance
To "progress", to "modernisation" –

What do you know of pavement or of machines?
What of the miles of neon lights
The sprawling centres "for sales and bargains"
That lie in wait
For your slow death?

No, it is useless,
Your self-knowing spirit has never dawned,
It is too late now
Your thighs are too old to remember your conquests;
How can I glorify you in the poetry meant only for heroes
Now that you are debauched
It is hardly necessary for me to remain faithful!

II.

Still, like the crazy lover that I am,
The old memories of our young nights
Seduce my heart's rancour.
My family lived here,
And my mother's family
The past lives in the hearts of old people. . .

My grandmother who died from exhaustion
Stealing a life for herself from poverty
Could neither read nor write, but sang
The old songs to the gas-lamps, and as a child
I sniffed the sharp smell of kerosene,
Mixed with the plaintive songs. . .
They were poor, they did what they could
In the basse ville, my grandmother
Sent out her prettiest daughters
To the butcher for meat.
"Do what you can" – the whispered password –
And can there be any sin when
Children are starving? "Do what you can" –
But button your blouses if you meet the priest.

My mother's brother, at the age of thirteen,
Died from tuberculosis or goiter;
He wanted to be a saint – they had to stop him
From sleeping on a bed of nails he had built.
After his death, the priests voted in favour
Of his canonization. My grandmother preferred
Obscurity. . .

Another uncle has recently died;
In his youth, he was an artist,
He had hope and ambition; a sculpture of his
Won a first prize in New York (far horizon)
He studied aux Beaux-Arts until he got married
Then his wife insisted on a better life;
He sold his paintbox for china plates
And ended his life as a postman

My mother's sister was schooled for a month
In a convent, though her eyes were resentful
The sex-urge dominant
At night, she'd escape for better places
And the nuns found her habit in the chapel
Tucked behind the organ

My aunts are unhappily married
There is no priest in the family
Only one uncle remains

III.

Tell me in your turn, my half-brothers
How splendid the view of the Chateau looks
From the torn-down houses of the docks
Tell me of the magnificent porcelain up there
The lights that glitter like jewels
You see them as you look up through the laundry
That your wives hang on the clothes-lines

Speak the Séparatiste party-line
Speak any line at all
Explain the disparity to me
Do not forget your past

St-Jean de Baptiste passes
In slow, ornate procession
Along the old streets of Quebec
Especially in summer
The priests wear their robes
The American tourists
Ride the calèches.
Your sacred images
Are in the hands of moneymakers
And at this you cannot be passive

O my mother, my mother
In all this
In my city that is whore to the tourists
In my city where they sell the old people's
Rocking-chairs and crosses,
Remind me of the past
Resurrect the old bitterness
What else do the old people conceal
Behind their ancient
Resignation?

Brenda Fleet

To Mother, on a Winter Day

Snow falling at your window
Restores your delicacy. Light
Glows on your throat; you are
A visionary in a placid dream.

Now you fold your arms, contented.
Is it a conclusion that you feel?
How easily events slide into place!
How skilled your use of instruments!

For once, discard your tinsel trappings.
        The snow covers nothing.
I know the power coiled in your arms;
The struggle's between us still.

Mutely, you fasten your eyes upon me,
        My soul is locked.
Why do you lust for your share?
You imagine the snow has cleansed me!

Brenda Fleet

My poetry has been chiefly lyrical in form, but from my growing social and political awareness, I have been writing longer poems of a more socially committed nature.

My attitude towards my writing is best summarized in a quotation by Anais Nin:

I live in the world made by the artists, for the other is full of horror and I can see no remedy for it.

Poetry is my moment of honesty, my personal refusal to compromise my truth. What I say in my poems has no doubt hurt people's feelings and caused me enemies. But this is the price I agree to pay. I have no time for diplomacy because there is no time left! Too much diplomacy, too many soft smiles, have perhaps put the human race in its present predicament. We write to try to rebuild.

Gail Fox

Poem for Rilke

"*in the deepest and
most important things,
we are unutterably alone*"

The bones of tiny birds
are perilous in their beauty.
They join to nothing,
know no hunger,
yet demand from us
forgotten wings, feathers
harsh riddles of eyes.

All we have is our solitude,
taken from the children
we were, who stoned
birds down to reach them better.

Dying, they drew
their breath
from desolate places.

Gail Fox

Lines for Ohiyesa, the Sioux

"*All who have lived
much out of doors, know
that there is a magnetic
and nervous force that
accumulates in solitude*"

You are alone
in forests

the snow is quiet
there are trees

there is nothing
like emptiness

anywhere

you walk
with no words

even shadows
are more than darkness

skin floats
on the bones of stars

your dream
returns

over and over

Gail Fox

Stones

Stones tumble and balance
in my hands, sheer force
from my fingers
controls their inclinations,
clicks their smooth
hard surfaces together,
divides them until again
they meet and shatter
the stillness of the lake,
the beach, the uncontrollable
movements of my past.

I think I was only ten
and he had but two years to live.
Together those two years,
we circled the ponds
and combed the open fields
for rocks, minerals,
fossils, things to speculate upon,
to touch, to chip open,
to reveal what we didn't know.
When he died,
I threw my rocks away,
forgot their names,
the way they looked and felt.

Today I hold a handful
of grey stones, meaningless
objects that I can control,
dead weights upon my living.

Gail Fox

My poems are generally short lyrics, products of a single fast inspiration that says what it says and finishes. No complexities. My longest poem consists of many small parts unified more by feeling than by imagery or subject.

Poems that describe, but fail to enter in, do not interest me. I think the poet has an almost moral obligation to disclose his feelings in a poem. How one can be a neutral poet today is unintelligible to me. Everything should be considered both within and without the personal experience.

Often people say that confessional poetry is neurotic. How inappropriate. Poems either work or they don't. The subject material is irrelevant. Some poets write about toothbrushes. Others about Greek myths. I would like to write about the experience of being a woman without using the traditional lady writer categories of wife, mother or frustrated daughter. When I can get beyond.

Dana Fraser

us in canada

cat cums sneekin
down   the   wawk
wat
or whoooom   duz
cat stalk?

cat meerlee   wants
to tawk
        klaw   at the
birdnecksdoor

*Statement

i try for a certain iconoclastic clarity to synthesize experience
as a person and a Canadian. am engaged in an ongoing process
of experimentation with forms of (poetic) communication and
have not isolated or developed a specific form in which i can
work most effectively. have not aligned myself with any particular
group and vacillate tremendously among being imagistic, sur-
realistic, symbolistic and realistic or even concrete. i guess i am
wherever the poem i am working on is. about the only thing
my productions have in common is that they are usually instigated
by a degree of personal horror in one form or another.

Gary Geddes

Swan Song

Ten years ago, standing
on a rock on Texada,
watching two drunks set out
in a gill-netter for Westview,
beer in one hand, helm in the other,
snatches of Annie Laurie caught
in the wind.
          A mile out,
the mast a crazy metronome
          cutting the air,
they turned over and were gone,
the barnacled hull glistening
          for a moment
like a blackfish in the sunlight.
I must have stood there an hour,
feeling myself too small an audience
          for their last great binge.

Gary Geddes

All of my most vivid memories are associated with the west coast of Canada, where I camped as a kid, worked, fished. Since those days I have been beached in institutions of higher learning, exchanging banalities and apprenticing for the business of Kultur.

I guess that poetry is a survival technique for me, a way of holding on to my sensations and impressions in this mad race to destroy the world that engages what's left of the imaginations of our leaders.

C. H. Gervais

Page from the Family Tree

the beginning pages
are filled with antoinette's
casket moving thru the
aisles of ste. anne's

& an ornate cross
gleaming in père renaud's hands
who stands with galoshes on
close to the open grave;

donalda's weeping for her dead
girl is not remembered in words,
nor is omèr's cross, it was built
for his dead sister from two

sticks found in the barn; donalda
burned the cross in the wood
stove promising her son (of 3 yrs.)
that it would be for antoinette

– from births & deaths of my
family, collected by my uncle; now
his death is written here with a
ballpoint pen below a photograph –:

the bottom of his cassock
caught by a wind, exposing his ankles
& shoes, standing in front of a
ramshackle house like a farm girl

C. H. Gervais

*Statement

Looking back (in a letter): "An old bum wearing oven mits in
the middle of winter once told me of a sunset and he related it
to me slowly, disjointedly, almost incoherently and said it better
than William Carlos Williams could ever explain it because the
bum felt it for the moment in just the same way he felt the cold of
that very day. You see, the true poet is the guy in the streets,
who is snug in the street, who is snug with a cup of coffee, who is
snug with the steps of a library, who doesn't read, who doesn't
want anything but just to flow like a sewer and a river at the same
time, who knows there's no such thing as a written poem. OK?"

Howard Halpern

BUMP

TODAY
I BUMP INTO A FRIEND
WHO I NOTICED
(NOT TOO LONG AGO)
SOLICITING $.$$
FROM STUDENTS OF YORK UNIVERSITY
FOR BIAFRA

NOW I SAY TO HIM:
I DIDN'T KNOW YOU
WENT IN FOR STUFF
LIKE THAT

HE SAYS, YEAH
I'M TAKING AN INTEREST
IN WHAT'S HAPPENING
OUT IN THE WORLD

I SAY, GROOVY
AND I ASK HIM
HEY, ARE YOU GOING TO
MARCH
WITH THE GEEKS
ON SATURDAY

HE SAYS
YOU MEAN
VIETNAM

I SAY
YEAH

HE SAYS, MAN, ARE
YOU KIDDING
SATURDAY IS MY BIRTHDAY, AND
I'M HAVING A PARTY
COME OVER
AND WE CAN WATCH IT
ON THE NEWS
AFTER THEY DO
THE BIT
ABOUT THE FIGHTING

BUT HERE
I SCRATCH MY HEAD
I DON'T KNOW
WHAT TO SAY
BECAUSE
I WAS PLANNING
TO GO, MYSELF,
AND MARCH

I MIGHT, AFTER ALL,
GET ON
TV
JESUS
I HOPE SO
MY FRIEND
WOULD BE
JEALOUS
AS ALL
HELL

10/25/68

Howard Halpern

When I write a poem, I want to say something. Something that everybody feels but nobody gets around to saying. My tools are words or letters and the printed page. I like words that evoke sharp, clear images. Zap! An immediate response.

If there is anything that distinguishes poetry from prose it is that the poet cares how his words appear on the page. The poem, for me, is a picture.

My aim is to give you just enough so that you'll want to come back for more.

David Helwig

After the Deaths at Kent State

          Today I see
gardeners in a formal garden
in a far country, here in England
surrounded by spring, by gentleness
and the smell of the green growth.

(A girl so thin I can see each muscle
move as she moves, walks
through the garden, writing in a book.)

In a shop, a man diseased appears to dance
behind me, all around the shop. I hold the hand
of a child that is not my own and think
of the far away dead, for them
there are no gardens.

David Helwig

The Children

We made them in the night,
unknowing, riding into time,
our minds on love or pleasure
or the darkness of the dark.

They were always unintended,
like beauty or like joy,
yet now they are my life
and time and place of being.

They are riding into time
on the dangerous ships of love.
They are riding into time,
into dark, into themselves.

We made them in the night,
and at the end we leave them,
leave them riding into time
in the darkness of the dark.

A Footnote to the Election

For John Diefenbaker

Once more into the confusion
of ballots and placards and slogans
that fly around my head like mad birds,
comes, ominous and insistent, the voice
of the man that no cartoonist
could have invented,
Zeus with tin thunder
the mad old man of the West
predicting storms.

In 1958 I was too young to vote
but walked the streets of Toronto
on election day for a candidate who lost
(like everyone else that year)
to the words of the visionary huckster.

I have never voted for him or his party
but tonight stare into the blur of television
and marvel again at his inevitable survival,
at the voice that can rejoice more in defeat
than most others in victory.

I will remember him
whether I want to or not,
as if he were a nightmare
or the kind of tune
that you can't get out of your head.

There are worse ways to go down
than as a bad old man
proud in his righteousness
and refusing everything but homage.

(And in a dozen years, in school
one of my children will probably be bored
with details of his years,
while out on the prairies
a thousand old tin cans
will lie in the stiff grass
behind a thousand empty shacks

and from the mouth of each
to the mad ears of withered men
will sometimes come the voice of an old thunder).

David Helwig

Balearic Winter

        All afternoon, the wind
has come from the sea to beat on the white walls
 of the island. The trunks of the Balearic pines
are bent by its force, and all day long
 I've thought of Chopin wintering on Majorca,
setting on paper the dainty marvels of his brain
 while the delicate webbed grip of his lungs
on the precious air grew slack and shallow,
 and he coughed, tried not to breathe, listened to rain.

 Outside this room, the wind is fast and loud
against the window and against the door
 that leads to our balcony. I sink in a chair
to work in the half light and whistle between my teeth
 a Chopin nocturne.

        In the mornings here
the young *emigrés* from Europe and America
 sit outside a bar in the main square
or walk through the narrow white streets of the old city
 past doorways that lead to dark small rooms and windows
where caged birds sing. A boy and girl will sit
 in shelter against a wall eating an orange.

Beside the road, daisies with yellow centres
 and single scarlet poppies are growing wild
among the almond trees, and by a white house
 the orange trees are thick and bright with fruit.

 In the afternoon, children walk on the beach
to gather shells, the miraculous common harvest
 of the shore, cowries, starfish, and all
the delicate architecture that is made
 and dies in the body of the sea, that children
wise and willful, gather in the lust of beauty
 and carry away, carrying to closed rooms
the faint smell of the sea.

                              Beside this sea
     shut up on Majorca, Chopin coughed in the rain
of the Balearic winter, an *emigré* writing down
     melodic effete nocturnes and songs in praise
of Poland where he did not live. While Sand
     comforted him and smoked and brooded and worked.

     Late in the afternoon, the sun, bright as a poppy,
drops westward to the Atlantic, always westward,
     like the gold that tempted west the burning eyes
of the conquistadors. Falling always, the sun
     drops into the ocean, under the Atlantic
to the golden sensual underwater cities
     that hang on the branches of the sea like oranges.

As the white walls darken and the island loses its gold,
     the *emigrés* smoke drugs in tiny rooms.
I drink white wine and coffee, and I think
     of those dainty effeminate fingers playing nocturnes
through all the wind and rain and fear of death
     of that Majorcan winter.

Ibiza, February 1970

David Helwig

Resolution

To write you no more poems.
No more, I tell myself, no more.
But still the words come out
as once, as ever, as now.

I came to where I am
by growing where you were.
I sometimes find your words
are on my lips.

But you are gone,
you have your love,
and I perhaps exaggerate
as lovers do
to prove that they
are there at all.

Yet say again
that where I go on being
whatever it is I am,
you are there, you are there.

David Helwig

A woman I was talking to last week tried to convince me that writing poetry was just as significant as living, was living, in fact, but I couldn't really buy that. No, not really.

Yet I'm glad that my poetry has been written, and many a dark time has been relieved by pen and paper. And the good times? Perhaps those are relieved too, for the pressure of joy and the pressure of pain are not all that different.

My poetry is a by-product, something that's created by the process of going on with whatever is there to go on with.
Or.
My poetry is what I write because I can't explain why I write poetry.
Or.
My poetry is what I write in case there's somebody listening.

A woman I was talking to last week tried to convince me that writing poetry was as good as living, was living, in fact. Before that she'd been talking about suicide.
My poetry is a search for grace.

I love writing poetry. If I thought it mattered I might not love it any longer.
My poetry is what I couldn't say.

A woman once quoted me an old Indian saying, "To name a thing is to create it." Then she told me she didn't believe that. I believed it.

My poetry is what I give you when you read it.

Bill Howell

After finally Reading Camus through to the End

All you great old men, sick
and stomping around your hermitages
like greater wounded bears,
drinking quart after quart of the basic acids,
belching Life with a capital "if"
and lurching through the last of it,
for the record, you're wrong.

As soon as you say "I think", you're gone.

Ah, so when you get old
you get selfish, eh?
And after a lifetime habit of giving?
Don't give me that!

My old man told me something once,
and for that once I was actually listening.
It was when I was at the rejecting everything stage,
you know, God and Jesus and the Church,
and split level homes and second cars and TV sets,
and first cars and TV sets, and everything,
and he said this: "If
you can't figure out what's what,
the hell with it. What's more important
is what you're going to do. Just do
what you feel is right, and what
you feel is good."

So I went downstairs to the basement
and grabbed ahold of my shirt
and found myself.
And came back up again.
And it was a long way both ways,
but here I am.

For the record again, I'll tell you all how
I'm going to end:
I'm ninety-seven
in my Ferrari on an Alpine roadway (or equivalents)
when I miss a hairpin
turn with my sixth or seventh wife, age 18,
beside me (again, or equivalents),
when a ball of living fire
crowns my charisma.

But you won't be around to see it, will you?

And all the headlines'll scream
"HOWELL'S VIRILITY REDUCED!" or "INTERNATIONAL
    STUD DUST!"
And everybody'll shake their head sadly
and smile and say I died
best. . .
        Once more, with feeling!

Bill Howell

Prometheus, 1957

Brian Atkinson was Wayne's older
brother, and it was when we were eleven,
and Brian aspired to climb where he wasn't allowed to go
up the DANGER – HIGH VOLTAGE tower
by the woods by the tracks late
one Saturday morning some seventy feet up
and we all heard
                        when he slipped and grabbed power in
an arc of jabbering humming light looking up there
and shrank so small that when we went to see where
his body had fallen, the indent hole in the ground
was about the same size as a baby's body,
and we all heard how he was burned to a crisp
at school that Monday, and everyone knew
Wayne that much better.

First Poem for another Woman

I am the man your last lover warned you about.

Our love will become the warmed-over memory of last night's
curry dinner, because I'll tell you inevitable lies.

I will even buy you lunch again at the *Hind Quarter*
so you can stare back at me and notice my impeccable
table manners, but I'll never tip the waitress.

I will marvel you with more inventive stories, packed
with convincing details, to make myself more of an enigma
to you.

I will get out of bed in the middle of the night
and write poems about you to persuade both of us
that you are the loveliest woman in the world.

                                        You will be
convinced that I'm the noblest, honestest
man in the world, even if you know I'm only that way
with you.

        I will tell you I love you because I don't
know where what comes out of me comes from.

                                        I will push
to lose myself in you, but I'll be painfully gentle,
because I'll be more afraid of what we might find out
than you.

        I will probably try to see God in your eyes
when I'm propped up on my elbows and moving slowly in
and out of you.

        I will close my eyes and make your
shoulder raw with my beard when I bury my head there,
and my sweat will smell like a man's sweat to you.

You will drown the bed with your love for me, and I
will spit myself into your pillow.

                                I will try not to
dream or hope too much for you, and I will tell you I love you
because I do, and your last lover will be right.

Bill Howell

And then the Morning Found Us

Breakfast, with fresh
frozen orange juice, as much
(someone told me once that half
the vitamin C is gone after ten
minutes, gets contaminated
by the day) as we want
for now.

(So what's the difference between
pollution and contamination
at this point?)

"May I *please* shave while you
are in there pissing?" (Words,
it seems, have habits, too.) Only
it never comes out like that.
It never comes out at all, sits there
with a cigarette and the juice taste
(vitamin C disintegrating, God I
know it, in my mouth) surrounded
by dirty dishes I might be washing
or at least rinsing, searching
for another better tomorrow
that just might be today, waiting
with no plans or serious
objections.

Bill Howell

Anthem

And men all over the world
  asked their women to dance
    for them.

And with song it was said,
  for there is nothing closer
    to your soul than your breath.

*Statement

One wonders who I am. And that's the starting point, the need
to find out what's coming and going inside myself, and in
the world around me. Outside that, I write so that people will
like me, and because I really dig it. I have a terrific com-
pulsion to try to tell incomplete strangers what I don't know. It's
as complex as that. And I've discovered, so far at least, that
people will like you if you do what you believe in. So I write as
an act of faith, I guess, so I can believe in myself. More and more
I find I have to live up to what I'm writing.

There are three impossible themes to render – physical love,
physical pain, and death. If you want to find out how good a writer
really is, look at what he shows you about these. They're all
lashed to the study of the workings of the human heart, which is
what writing is all about. I find the biggest hassle is self-
discipline, and trying to remember that I'm not the Eighth Wonder
of The World. I have to work like hell for everything I get.
For me, a poem isn't worth a damn unless you can see some of
the poet's blood, right there on the page. And someday I hope
to write a poem in which I don't lie, even a little bit.

Patrick Lane

Wild Horses

Just to come once alone
to these wild horses
driving out of high Cascades,
raw legs heaving the hip-high snow.
Just once alone. Never to see
the men and their trucks.

Just once alone. Nothing moves
as the stallion with five free mares
rushes into the guns. All dead.
Their eyes glaze with frost.
Ice bleeds in their nostrils
as the cable hauls them in.

Later, after the swearing
and the stamping of feet,
we ride down into Golden:

'Quit bitchin.
It's a hard bloody life
and a long week
for three hundred bucks of meat.'

That and the dull dead eyes
and the empty meadows

Patrick Lane

Ten Miles in from Horsefly

Ten miles in from Horsefly,
shoulders sore from my pack,
feet blistered, I asked
and got a job cleaning a barn
for the price of a meal
and the promise I could sleep
outside the unseasonal rain
and worked like a damn
as digger flies took chunks
of meat from my arms
and mosquitoes sucked my blood.

No one knows how far an hour goes
or how short are the days —
shovelling ten months of shit
from a barn clears your head
and allows you to look forward
to sleep without fear or favour
from old sad dreams of enemies
and friends. Just to have one moment
with shoulders clear of weight
and feet braced finally still
as you come breathless
to the clear hard boards below.

Patrick Lane

The Sun Has Begun to Eat the Mountain

Pines eat mist out of the sky
in the village the old
man with yellow eyes
lies stretched out on the mat
he is dying

Stones change shape as they breathe
in the bush the shaman
scrapes the green bark
from the devil's club
she will purge death
again this spring

Birds are silent when day ends
in my silence
I wonder again at the far cities
tell me again
the story of the beginning

You who are near enough to death
please tell me
where the beginning is
look
the sky weeps
the woman comes

Tell me where the sun goes
when the mountains are all eaten
and the world is only a flatness
where eagles fly
cutting the sky to ribbons
with their great wings

Patrick Lane

*Statement

Last surviving remnant of Lane tribe who wanders poem in pocket
looking for ultimate handout from God who doesn't listen wise
old apocalyptic Spirit drunk in some celestial temple ignoring pain
and raving words the poems of mine like the fist in my face
I got last week in beerparlour and now blind without my glasses
I hide in my room with vorpal typewriter cunningly mapping
revenge stumbling in street over the helpless bodies of nuns I've
attacked thinking them tough Italian hoods or celebrating falling
leaves imagining sky falling on me chicken little seeking the
ultimate answer the poems all out of the distances travelled
the spaces in between the mad sad lost last wilderness everywhere
around me on the street or in the bush wherever pedants
gather to push back the curtain of darkness I am there to wrap it
around me and stand the fool at the gate with Cerebus snap-
ping at my heels a mirror shield in my hand while the antigravity
belt around me fails and I fall into hissing snakes trying to
remember where I lost my glasses tying my shoes to my fly so
I'll die with my boots on struggling to reconcile myself with
the lady dancing in the light of a Blue Cafe yelling over my tenth
beer I can't see I can't see and then writing a poem about it
putting it in an empty bottle and throwing the whole shiteroo at
the moon.

Dennis Lee

1883

The Compact sat in parliament
To legalize their fun.
And now they're hanging Sammy Lount
And Captain Anderson.
And if they catch Mackenzie
They will string him in the rain.
And England will erase us if
Mackenzie comes again.

The Bishop has a paper
That says he owns our land.
The Bishop has a Bible too
That says our souls are damned.
Mackenzie had a printing press.
It's soaking in the Bay.
And who will spike the Bishop till
Mackenzie comes again?

The British want the country
For the Empire and the view.
The Yankees want the country for
A yankee barbecue.
The Compact want the country
For their merrie green domain.
They'll all play finders-keepers till
Mackenzie comes again.

Mackenzie was a crazy man,
He wore his wig askew.
He donned three bulky overcoats
In case the bullets flew.
Mackenzie talked of fighting
While the fight went down the drain.
But who will speak for Canada?
Mackenzie, come again.

Dennis Lee

Third Elegy

It would be better maybe if we could stop loving the children
and their delicate brawls, pelting across the square in tandem,
        deking
from cover to cover in raucous celebration and they are never
winded, bemusing us with the rites of our own
gone childhood; if only they stopped
mattering, the children, it might be possible, now
while the square lies stunned by noon.
What is real is fitful, and always the beautiful footholds
crumble the moment I set my mind aside, though the world does
        recur.
Better, I think, to avoid the scandal of being – the headlong
particulars, which as they lose their animal purchase
cease to endorse us, though the ignominious hankerings
go on; this induces the ache of things, and the lonesome ego
sets one once again dragging its lethal desires across the world,
which does not regard them. Perhaps we should
bless what doesn't attach us, though I do not know
where we are to find nourishment.
So, in the square, it is a
blessed humdrum: the kids climb over the Archer, and
the pool reflects the sky, and the people passing by,
who doze, and gently from above the visible pollutants descend,
coating the tower's sheath. Sometimes it
works but once in summer looking up I saw the noxious cloud
        suspended
taut above the city, clenched, as now everywhere it is the
imperial way of life that bestows its fall-out. And it did not
stay inert, but across the fabled horizon of Bay Street they
came riding, the liberators, the deputies of Jesus, the Marines,
and had released bacterial missiles over the Golden Horseshoe for
        love of all mankind,
and I saw my people streaming after calling welcome for the small
        change,

91

and I ran in my mind crying humiliation upon the country,
as now I do also for it is
hard to stay at the centre when you're
losing it one more time, though the pool
reflects the placid sky, and the people passing by, and daily
our acquiescence presses down on us from above and we have no
        room to be.
It is the children's fault as they swarm for we cannot stop caring.

In a bad time, people, from an outpost of empire I write
bewildered, though on about living. It is to set down a nation's
failure of nerve; I mean complicity, which is signified by the
gaseous stain above us. For a man who
fries the skin of kids with burning jelly is a
criminal. Even though he loves children he is a criminal. Even
        though his
money pumps your oil he is criminal, and though his
programs infest the air you breathe he is
criminal and though his honest quislings run your
government he is criminal and though you do not love his
        enemies
he is criminal and though you lose your job on his say-so he is
criminal and
though your country will founder without him he is criminal and
though he has transformed the categories of your
refusal by the pressure of his media he is a criminal.
And the consenting citizens of a minor and docile colony
are cogs in a useful tool, though in no way
necessary and scarcely
criminal at all and their leaders are
honourable men, as for example Paul Martin.

In Germany, the civic square in many little towns is
hallowed for people. Laid out just so, with
flowers and fountains, and during the war you could come and

relax for an hour, catch a parade or just
get away from the interminable racket of the trains,
clattering through the outskirts with their lousy expendable cargo.
Little cafes often, fronting the square. Beer and a chance to relax.
And except for the children it's peaceful here
too, under the sun's warm sedation.

The humiliations of imperial necessity
are an old story, though it does not
improve in the telling and no man
believes it of himself.
It is not Mr. Martin who sprays the poison mist
on the fields of the Vietnamese, not in person nor fries civilians
       and if he
defends an indefensible war, making himself a
stooge, making his people accessories to genocide, he is no
worse a man than the other well-intentioned sellouts of history –
the Britons who went over to the legionaries, sadly for the sake
       of the larger peace,
the tired professors of Freiburg, Berlin, the statesmen at Munich,
       those
estimable men, and the lovers of peace, the brisk switchers who
told it in Budapest. Doesn't the
service of quiet diplomacy require dirty hands?
(Does the sun in summer pour its warm light into the square
for us to ignore? We have our own commitments.)
And then if it doesn't work one is finally
on the winning side though that is
unkind: Mr. Martin is an honourable man, as we are all
Canadians and honourable men.

And this is void, to participate in an
abomination larger than yourself. It is to fashion
other men's napalm and know it, to be a
Canadian safe in the square and watch the children dance and

dance and smell the lissome burning
bodies to be born in
old necessity to breathe polluted air and
come of age in Canada with lies and vertical on earth no man
            has drawn a
breath that was not lethal to some brother it is
yank and chink and hogtown linked in
guilty genesis it is the sorry mortal
sellout burning kids by proxy acquiescent
still though still denying it is merely to be human.

Thursday

Powerful men can lose it too. It is Thursday, a mean old lady
    has died, she got him his
paper route and there is still that whiff of
ju-jube and doilies from her front hall; a stroke; he can
taste them going soggy; anyway; some in his pocket too,
    they always picked up
lint; anyway, she is dead.
Next morning,
hacking the day into shape on the phone, there is no
way – routine & the small ache,
he cannot accommodate both.
At Hallowe'en too, in her hall.
And I know which one he takes and that
night at six, while the kids are
    tackling his legs with their small tussling,
how he fends them off, tells them "Play upstairs"; one day
they will be dead also with their jelly beans.
In her kitchen, she had a parrot that said "Down the hatch!"

Dennis Lee

More Claiming

That one is me too – belting through
    school to the rhythms of glory, tripping, blinking at vanishing
       place names
  Etobicoke   Muskoka   Labrador   Notting Hill Gate but he
    could
    never keep them straight
though as they ran together they always had
    people in them, like ketchup on his shirt.
  Extra-gang spikers and singalong, I believe that was
    Labrador?   Teachers.   That
girl in Stockholm – Christ! what did they
    expect? He was otherwise engaged.

For there were treks, attacks and
    tribal migrations of meaning, wow
careening thru his skull, the doves &
    dodos that descended, scary
partnerships with God, new selves erupting
    messianic daily – all the grand
adrenalin parade:
    he was supposed to wear matching socks?

It was a messy pubescent
    surfeit of selves but there were
three I didn't know about,
    the sabotage kids.
They never budged.
One was perpetually leaving his
    penis behind in garbage bags. One had a
bazooka stuck in his throat, hence had some
    difficulty speaking.
The third would sob all night in the lonesome night,
    crying for something damp, and close, and warm.

I came across them far too late.
    They kept on dousing
       epiphanies, misdirecting traffic.
    They kept on daring me to
       break down, like a carburetor with a passion for wildflowers.

Dennis Lee

*Statement

I've decided that the challenge for me is *not* to learn how to
project a Lee in the poems who is all Sensitive Plant, or all fuming
erection, or whatever variant of the Poet-as-Feelie is current.
The challenge is rather to learn to write poetry that can convey
a rich indistinction of passion, thought, feeling, whimsicality,
etc. in its own voice – since those things are all present, and all
inextricable, in my own way of marching through a day from
morning to night.

Can I make that clearer? I wanted the voice of the poems to say
things directly, concretely, with as much simplicity as is granted by
(say) clear eyesight. But the voice itself I wanted to be a rich
organic manifest of being human – so that it would become im-
possible to say, "This is the voice of a man who has a bunch
of feelings; or, of a man who is analyzing something; or, of a man
who (. . . fill in the blank)." What I wanted as response was,
"This is a human voice."

Bernell Macdonald

it is you that makes the song

it is no bird that sings the note you hear
    leave your ears to thunder
    your fingers to thorns
    your eyes to the stars
    your nose to the rose or other things
    that come by chance

a heart as delicate as a bird's very being
has power in the weather

through imitation it is you that makes the song

(the bird only knows where his own heart lies)

David McFadden

For Dwight D. Eisenhower on His Death

March 28/69

'We can't let those Communists take over in Viet Nam,'
he said, after the French were yanked,
'what would we do for tin & tungsten? (what the hell's tungsten)
We must set up a Pro-American Puppet Government
in Sigh-gone.' It made so much sense
& he was so honest.

                    He'd outlived his world
& didn't know it. He stepped out of
Gasoline Alley, Kansas, & it died behind him.
Gasoline Alley'd been cancelled by the Toronto Globe & Mail
a few months before his death – what would he have thought?

What were his secret thoughts on Allen Ginsberg?
Did he know anything about Marshall McLuhan?
'The medium is the message? That's pretty clever.'

A naked Viet Conger with a bomb strapped to his back
ran into an American compound & exploded
killing no one but himself, unknown, unnamed
& the next day Eisenhower was dead.

David McFadden

The Fiddlehead

(for Kitty)

O my life is so simple & the world
so unutterably complicated, like a kid
thinking about how the universe began.

Thinking about myself as well as I can
with the cat purring like a pneumatic drill
crawling around my head & shoulders

I'd say my head is empty as an old beer bottle
found in the woods, you pick it up curious
& get a faint whiff of last year's beer

& a strong sense of woodsy secrets,
the spiritual processes of trees, popping seedpods
the daily sun, rotting layers of loam

bottle like a discarded espionage device
anchored glumly in the swirling great joy.

David McFadden

Titles I Have Heard of but not Read

Dreams have become so full of perfect intricate detail
& yet evaporate upon getting up –
Went up in a balloon thousands of feet above
      the Niagara Peninsula
& jumped out with a parachute going down through
      cold wet clouds
& landing in Midway of country fair –
Went up again, took my father up this time,
he pretended amazement at how well I could handle
      balloon's controls –
meaningless dreams, just for fun.

& this would make a good short story:
Going through familiar territory & suddenly
came across a store, combination garage
      & general store
that I knew had been torn down 15 years ago –
Saw traffic but not much but what traffic
      there was:
cars over 20 years old looking new –
Garage was locked up, went into general
      store
& all the stuff just smelled & looked
      like 20 years ago,
remembrance of tiny things I'd never remember –
Checking prices, going through small wooden
      bins of perfect detail
detail so perfect I never dreamt I was dreaming,
I figured by some sad loop I'd landed in 1953,
asked the fat happy storekeeper's wife what year
      it was
& she threw her arms around me & laughed
& said You mean you don't know what year it is?
& then her daughter & son-in-law called out from
      the back room
It's 1949.

Later, Jack, Al & me drove around checking
      details of 1949
trying to make sure no one was playing an
      elaborate joke on us.
Went down to Lake Erie, water was clean,
      beach was clean –
Everywhere we went we questioned people,
      cross-examined them,
asked them if they'd ever heard of
      Elvis Presley,
hummed Let It Be for them, all of
      that,
went to a movie, sat in balcony
      of old-fashioned movie house
while old-fashioned horror movie was playing
& people fainting all around us.

Later went down to Joan's old neighborhood
around Barton & Kenilworth,
saw her young mother & father, happy in
      prime of life
then saw little Joan 9 years old sitting
      on curb
then went around to Main & Kenilworth
      looking for 9-year-old me,
4-year-old Jack & mom & dad in their
      early 30s –
Suddenly we were back in 1970 –

Oct. 12/70

101

David McFadden

A Representative of Violence

O Sunday morning in early April
the cat purring at my feet in hunger
no food in the house & Joan groaning
& the two kids looking at me

me with a stomach & head full of beer
on this day of Spring
with tulips greentips protruding
& some people buy artificial tulips
& stick them upright in their beds
like those nasty sneaky Negro blondes

& I am about to float out to my car
& slide through traffic to
        pick up a batch of hot food

        What'll it be? Teenburgers from the A & W
                (wch stands for Amburgs & Wootbeer)
        or Chinese food from Roy's
        or Italian food from Vista's?
        I wonder as I hop in car & can't decide
        & the car veers off straight for Vista's –

        I order three chicken noodle soups
                one small pizza double cheese
                one bag of lascagna double hot
        & the girl's sweater she can hardly breathe it's
                so tight & her red hair pluckt eyebrows
        & her plumpness so overbound

        Waiting, I pull out of my pants
        my copy of *The Double Helix*

        & coming in past me the people
                eager for hot food, overprepared
        & going out past me the sated
                newly amazed at the colours
                of a Spring afternoon, early Spring
                in the unbombed cities of the Great Lakes.

David McFadden

Just off the Junction of Hwys 8 and 20

Early Sunday morning I pull in for gas
& the gas jockey in his lean thirties, front tooth missing
has been sitting for hours, no customers,
quiet, no traffic – the faint sound of traffic
from the Queen Elizabeth Way three miles away
& a few birds chirping strangely.

  He's been sitting there reading, feet propped
  an interesting new big thick novel
  & looks at me with wide eyes
  & I feel myself slip in & out
  of his imagination.

    I turn off Queenston Road
    go down gravel-topped Kenora
    & look at some newly built homes for sale.
    Early Sunday morning nobody sees me
    looking in through vacant windows
    bending down to look through basement windows
    stand tiptoed to look through upper split windows
    try the locked doors, run fingers along wood trim
    smell deeply the new mortar.

        Very nice new homes in a good location
        Woods close by, easy access to expressway & city
        & I know the down payment & monthly payments &
        taxes would be too high.
                        Better by far
        be a penniless bum than a penniless homeowner.

David McFadden

*Statement

*A ferbile movement, lasting 24 hours and then disappearing,
may for convenience be called ephemeral fever; if of three or four
days' duration, febricula.*

I don't like making statements; it seems so pompous
and dull-witted to answer questions that haven't been asked.

*You can do nothing to bring the dead to life but you can do much
to save the living from death.*

Anthologies, even what Victor Coleman calls form-letter
anthologies, are like little sample displays you see at huge global
philatelic exhibitions. I like them when they are classified for
illumination or even convenience, but not when they're classified
for political purposes. I take a precious view of good poems;
they are like people and should not be ranked or pushed around.

*Clean, healthful exercise not only aids in the development of their
bodies but helps to keep their thoughts from wandering to
forbidden subjects.*

Poems will be spinning in space long after there is no more world,
or my name isn't

DAVID McFADDEN

Italicized items are from *Library of Health*, 1923.

Barry McKinnon

letter 11: for my wife

I return again
to the river
we walked to then
with the old indian blanket
your mother had placed away
in a closet
years before we borrowed it

then your hand led me
thru the streets and alleys
we had also touched in
toward the dark
trees to the south
to the river
running below the cliff

and the grass was high
so we crushed a nest in it
placed the old blanket down
and placed our bodies over the miniature tents
that strong grass pokes
in a thin blanket
and your hand was still
in mine

I remember
we waited for the sun
to go down
to sink away for the black privacy
we needed
but it never really
did get dark
and there were other voices
in the background of the poplar trees
people who should **not see**
or hear us

as we began (I slipping my pants
    down to my knees
and you I remember
had trouble your
eyes squinted shut
as if in pain
and my eyes squinting in the pain
I knew you would suffer
from

and the pain of later
walking back toward the rows of lights
and houses
still holding our new hands
almost 20 minutes older and unsure
of themselves
new and awkward smells clinging
to our bodies

and I remember
it was not beautiful
another lie someone had told
and I was on the edge of tears or fear
in the way you
talked of marriage
as if a debt
were to be paid
back

and the pain of later
trying to compose the perfect poem
of birds nests and smells and
and the beauty of skin etc
trying to forget that a stretched rubber
was not a monument

and the pain of later
I think I went back
to that place alone
but the grass had resumed its shape
and some children had found the thing
maybe to blow up with water
like I'd seen them do before

but the river still ran
below me
and I reconstructed the echoes
of your voice
pretending that I had made you
into a perfection or
that I had become old
with wisdoms

but it was not beautiful
and the lies were to my friends

it was not beautiful
but I had come
to love you

Barry McKinnon

the carcasses of spring

we found sections of spine
animal bones with black meat
bones protruding from
mud
      where grass had begun to grow

and coyotes at night
sneaking upon the remains
of winter. traces of blood left. covered
by another dark

and my grandmother old
with many deaths
and many explanations of it
feeding chickens
                      without concern

and we continuing beyond her
following the flight of a hawk
toward the coulee
                searching for
simple flowers
in some simple
            earth

Barry McKinnon

first confession is that I didn't learn the alphabet until grade three.
in high school I started to write poetry as an act of rebellion –
to claim an identity that was my own. I had the lowest mark in
latin (25%) and weighed 98 lbs. (honestly). I dropped out, as they
say, and started to write secret poetry in my basement room –
hours of scribbling magic lines that made no sense – that made
incredible sense – and would go to school feeling brilliant. la puella
est pulchra. the girl is beautiful, is the only latin I remember.

after high school I continued my joyous scribbling until the real
girl left me. the poetry got serious – that attempt to conjure
flesh with words – words to reclaim what you've lost – words to
carry the emotion and as final compensation, to make the pain
beautiful. but that indulgence changed as I continued to change.
now, I've come to the belief that the poet is the sophisticated
ad man (madman) who has special rhythmic news about the thing
we call the spirit and the forces that corrupt it.

Tom Marshall

Pub Talk

The vague, drunken girl who looked like a lesbian —
thick spectacles, close-cropped hair —
was found dead in her apartment. Where
she hoped to get to beyond reach
of her slick, moustached lover, friends, ex-husband
we do not know.
She was cadging drinks from us
one week ago.

Tom Marshall

Snow

Across the street a student
lobs snowball after
snowball at his friend's
(girl's) upstairs window.

My Singhalese
fishermen friends in their
watercolour sketches watch
in brown astonishment.

Tom Marshall

West Street

I woke up at midnight and heard him singing
the wooden owl above my balcony
at long last flying free
That owl-house my apartment was flying
the park outside singing in the midnight wind

Limestone and brickwork of Kingston sang
a high sweet song
till midnight was noon and gold sun shining
tumult in the willows their gold whips turning
into a kind of singing

The owl fierce with midnight song
the gold willow singing in the wild sunshine
limestone and park singing
about stone and gardens that live forever
by noon and midnight

Tom Marshall

*Statement

The poetry game, the artgame, operates like Tarot cards or the
Rorschach ink blot. With its patterning of thought, sound and
image it interprets us to ourselves – a rather necessary function.
Of course, some people would rather not know. But the forces
that destroyed Hiroshima and Nagasaki are not outside us. They
are inside us. We stand a slightly better chance of survival if we
are in touch with them.

Some of my poems have done this for me, and perhaps for
others. I would like now to write a more direct, fluid and clear
language than before in order to reach further in and also
farther out.

Sid Marty

Fox on the Wire

Where did you come from
red one
to dance upended
deadly still
in the south country
of Saskatchewan

A herd of deer
run the edge
of yellow stubble
All around
the purple crocuses
stretch to the Wood Mountain
over spring wet earth

Here on the nuisance ground
flowers bedeck a rusty ford
old cans full of sweet water
hold the sky, mirror your body

Your coat was prime and full
soft as new snow, red like autumn fire

Deer Lodge, Off Season

      I'm here to stand
      quietly now
      Where I once swam up
      the moonlight road at bay
      When I was the Warden
      at Takkakaw Falls
      and heard that water
      falling all the day

The fierce river at my cabin steps
That first threatened, and later
Bore me away, each night asleep
Rocking me under

I'd come in the night to my friend
In the midst of pressing his poems
On mulberry sheets, that looked
Like the woodchips from my axe

Having rested the bones of trees
With runes graven on cirque walls
He got out his bottles, the liquid
Brought forth swimming maidens

We drowned each one carefully
Twining rainbow trout and salmon
In their hair of black or golden
Then rescued them all, before

They floated into the world
And over Takkakaw Falls
That I might sleep
In the mountain night
Not to be out with the lantern
Scaring my horses with light

I'm here to stand quietly now
The first November avalanche
On Mount Victoria so far away
Breaks like a page
from this blue story
Into the legends of Abbot's Pass

Sid Marty

Night. Camp below Maligne Pass (Jasper Park)

Standing in the dark meadow
drinking coffee
The white bell mare
in mountain shadow
her bell clinking
a cold night in.
The stars
vastly
shine in the metal
A tame bull moose
wades through willow

Campfire lights up the tent
Woman throws a branch
on the fire
On the trail
is the five toed
track of a grizzly
"our brother across the river"
Horses think of 'mustahya'*
and of getting by me
Though they're hobbled
they've learned
to jump
their front feet
down the trail
to home

*Cree word for "mighty bear."

Sid Marty

Lightning Storm

The forestry line is shorted out
has been for weeks
Picking up the ear piece
we hear
a thousand birds on a wire
miles apart
each in separate song
I don't know how this can be
While somewhere a lynx growls
from a lodgepole pine
where a bird was singing
on an insulator

During the lightning storm
the bell rings slowly
on every strike
resistors smoke,
the line to Jasper is out
The district warden's 30 miles up
the Little Cairn river
hasn't been heard from
can't be reached

Twelve spruce have fallen
on the lines at Beaver Cabin
In the morning, we'll be climbing
splicing wire, cutting deadfalls
with the chainsaw

Answering the switchboards ring
I shout, "do you need help?"
Far away the faint voice
fades in the sound of lightning
sound of wild cats in the timber

Sid Marty

Each Mountain

> Each mountain
> its own country
> in the way a country
> must be
> A state of mind

News of the mountains
brought out by the horse guides
long time ago, though some old boys
live long, tell it still in legion halls
how they cut trails to the high tundra
packing a few adventurers
through deadfall of the timber bands
last of the taiga
to find their way
bright with wild cranberry
and flowers

Each mountain
where local climate
controls the shade
of paintbrush and anemone
Colours and moods
vary as the weather, suddenly.

But we belonged here too
men and women
our loving squalls
intemperate desires
wide ranging
hot and cold
like August glaciers
as we travelled for pleasure
walking above the trees
and climbing the summits

Because the smell
of wild mountain flowers
of a thousand hues
threatened the civilized monster
carried in us from the highway

Must be tempered
with the threat of loss
Thus we gain
romantics because
each mountain
made us so
would not have us
any other way

Sid Marty

Routine

Moose runs out from the salt lick
as I amble toward the corral
a great silent shadow
with a silver tree for a head

Yesterday, he put the run on the woman
when she raised her voice to him
and when she retreated giggling,
behind a tree
he thot this mockery of his bent face
and leaped, standing, over a four foot fence
graceful as a giant gazelle

I almost catch his scent
as he waits upwind
graciously
while I piss beside the manger
talking to the mare
who expertly blocks the gelding
from getting his share of the hay
by laying back her ears
and shifting her hind legs
threateningly towards him

The mare's in heat
and though she kicks and nips him daily
the gelding's revenge is poetic
So unfair, that I consider
planting a salt block
in the corral

That old six pointer
might just bust in here
cover the mare for us
in the process of being
worth his salt

It would be
a cheap thrill for me
breaking my routine
to see a wild Canadian beast
domesticated so
(moose moving closer now)
pausing at my growing
man made salt lick, which
hey!
might be dangerous
for me too, come to think of it

Sid Marty

Th Pocohontas Kid

Th Pocohontas Kid
was the handle, hung
on a young Warden
in Pocohontas district

A palpable title
as the kid's voice
quivering on the radio was
"Worried about a flat tire"
they said, "or some knothead
five minutes late
from a mountain climb"

The kid's voice
giving off bad vibrations
amid the silence of the pine
and heat waves
smoke of forest fires
distant, and too terrible
to contemplate

His tenor, rising a pitch
could bring tears of commiseration
"th sad son-of-a-bitch"
they might say, looking off
to distant hazy vistas
to fire lookouts
choking blind in smoke
impotent

Wishing they could
turn off the radio
"Jesus Christ"
they would swear softly
in the midst
of shoeing a horse

122

Swatting huge
steak eating flies
amid horse farts
"Jesus Christ"
they would say
The kid's voice echoing
in a distant truck

Sid Marty

So we walked across the CPR bridge and the poet said "I don't want to always have the poem pointing out my life like a double barrelled shotgun"; at which point, by arrangement with his personal magus, four mule deer does broke out of willow cover in the coulee. Springing over the high buck brush, they jumped fences, ran over the prairie towards the safety of the city. It is hunting season.

"Linear speech has trapped us, forced the poet's ideas to mount each other, couple indecently, cramped in sharp corners. Discard syntax," he gesticulated. At the motion, a covey of partridge plunged out of some rose bush. I raised my arms on reflex to take aim; no shotgun.

Four urchins rode by on four gradations of cheval, inversely proportional to the size of urchin rider, and we coughed politely in their dust, saying nothing. Talked of the poem on a cylinder that went round the world, and in its new arrangement, once cut a house in half. Talked of the form of the poem, as always exceptionally open to genius or abuse.

We walked around on the groundwork of our beloved whore, fallen lady, prying into crevices, exterminating exotic viruses. We wanted to revive her. I wrote a song about her, put it in a folder with the others. Poetry and the song attempt to be separate, but they keep merging into each other when I pick up a guitar. I wrote a song about the country that wants to become a poem, wrote a letter about it. That seems to be all for now.

David Phillips

the conversation

i think a conversation
connects
              my friends necks
stick out of envelopes &
speak
              their own concerns
brought near
                  & dear to me

their words
such different shades

a painting
              in the parts
my own replies

a kind of collage
moving
          thru various post offices

timed

the news collects us
all
    in my head
the words dance

the conversation
taken up/
          left here & there
across the country
all of us
          speaking our hearts out

                              may 70

David Phillips

Perhaps writing is like running down or up a hill; an activity. i
also agree communication is involved. i like the idea of the poem
being a means of transport – as if it is, at the same moment, the
telegram & the means of sending it. its messages. whose ideas are
these? are all these ideas merely in the way of our seeing the
poem? it seems a matter of access to the poem & each of us has
access to certain poems at certain times, & some poems have
to be left until yu suddenly find yourself reading them.

Marc Plourde

for Monnie

I can't find her eyes
they move away
then back again

now she's imitating animals
& insects
and bends over the table
squealing in someone's ear

her friends laugh
but just out of politeness,
they don't like her stupid jokes

she's embarrassing
even dangerous
what if the cops
came into this coffee shop

we'd get busted
because of her
an eighteen-year-old

who's been taking drugs:
pot speed hash acid,
she mixes them together

too bad for us all
that she had a kid
three months ago
and it's in some orphanage

as it is I don't think
she'll last three more months,
everyone in the place is nervous
and looking around

at the other end of the table
Monnie goes on giggling
& making wild faces

Andrew Suknaski

Goya

by Andrei Voznesensky

I am Goya!
The raven pecked out my eyes,
                     I who fell on the stripped-field.
I am misfortune.

I am voice
of War, the heads of cities
                     on snow of 1941.
I am famine.

I am a throat
of the hanged-woman whose bell-like body
                     rang across a barren marketplace . . .
I am Goya.

O frosted-grapes
of retribution! To the West –
                     I threw the ashes
                     of your unwanted visitor!
And I beat, as nails, the sound stars
into the eternal heaven.
I am Goya.

1970

Andrew Suknaski

Eternal Triangle

the warm empty bus
   was hurling itself at the arms
      of night   you were shivering

as i said good night
   half-jealous   half-caring that you
     with a coin in hand

would share your last smile
   with the lonely driver this night
     as he gave you change

Andrew Suknaski

Woman

a woman
gathers
rhubarb
  at
     the
       edge
         of
           forest

she carries
a basket
       on
       top
       of
       her
       head

her rueful
glance
as she
passes
reminds me
of my
brother
who told
stories
about
korean women
who carried
ceramic vessels
of water
the same way
as soldiers
used beautiful
pottery
for target
practice
and sometimes
missed

Andrew Suknaski

Hitch-Hiking

that spring
I remember
how the cold nightwind
knifing the prairie
somewhere south
of north battleford
poisoned me.

each hour added
another spoon of hate
to my marrow
as I became more
violent – cursing
every truckdriver
that passed me.

i know that
if the world
had been a single brick
about that time,
one karate blow
propelled by the helium
of my hate
would have cracked it
in half.

and then a truck stopped –
that very moment
i could have become
a downright bootlicker.

i could have curled
the dust
on that man's boots
into a nightingale
which might have flown
away with the first
puff of air
as his foot tramped
the gas pedal to the floor.

Andrew Suknaski

My poems are not my life; they are not even part of my life. A
poem is a sniper ready to assassinate everything worth believing
in – or living for. The logic of poems and men is capable of
anything – even genocide. I would not want anyone to make his
life a poem (or a novel), that could only end in the creation of
a way of life where one moves like a Frankenstein monster. Do
not believe in my poems, or ideas therein – if there are any, do
not believe what I write at this moment – even suspect yourself at
this moment if you feel yourself moving into another conscious-
ness. If my poems can possibly make you feel uneasy (even cons-
cious of your consciousness), then that is all that matters.

For 22 years I have moved from room to room in a few schools
and universities whose teachers proposed to educate me; mov-
ing, and growing lonelier than Judas after the kiss, among those
masses of people, I suspect I may have been de-educated –
and may have to spend the next 28 years of my life, now 28, trying
to find my heart and soul. If I could have the chance to betray
myself again, I would learn the alphabet at thirty-three, after
listening to grizzlies turn stones for ants in the high mountains
where, of course, I would have worked as an illiterate mountain
guide living on goat's milk and wine.

Tom Wayman

The Dow Recruiter, *or*
This Young Man Is Making Up His Mind

They're always playing tricks on me, by
telling me their name is Eichmann, or
they're really interested in our
gas project – the one for Zyklon-B.
Others are earnest, showing me those –
those photographs of the children and
appealing to me as a man, how
can one work for the company if
it is like that. Others say the creeps
outside don't bother them, they just want
to work for something settled, with plans.
And there are those who take the folders
thoughtfully, as I did, thinking too
of the God-damned crying child.
                                                    Flowers,
bright red ones along the lane, turn just
one side to the sun, one face of their
mass of petals. What a man is, is
less clear, and what a man is doing . . .
Violence overflows, the shouting and
the bodies crowd in sometimes, the red-
faced officials saying things to me
and all those people. My wife keeps our
bedsheets cool and quiet, now that the
money comes. Sundays, the green spread and
the white room hold the lights, and outside
red flowers are growing in the lane.

Tom Wayman

December

In the papers
an oil tank burns at El Segundo
and a girl is jailed for fifteen days.

All day the smoke drifts south
thinning into a huge layer
over the Christmas freeways and the tracts and palms.

In October, her name
was only one of our busted and bailed.
And then she was: at meetings
a voice so heavy that it breaks sometimes,

an invitation at Thanksgiving –
no more than a flash and a glow of
loveliness, through the dull slough
of days of expectation gently unfulfilled

and friends dying of time, or chemicals
or nothing more important than despair . . .
Anyway, after arguing through her prison night
that the wine is good, that our individual tragedies
are inevitable against the historical one,
back under the moon, the smell of oil
like touring between the steel decks of a warship,
the smell of oil.

Tom Wayman

Despair

DOW appears and the poet Robert Bly,
and a building is taken and lost –
Colorado State University, November 1968

I

As though something knew Bly was coming
the night he arrived the first snow began
to sign wearily down on
the building we argued in
down on the humps in the parked streets,
on houses.
At the edge of town: cold fields
where we found sadness in cabin lights
being forced unhappily out onto the white ground.
We loaded the truck with black boards for
barricades, from the floor of an old silo,
breathing the new winter around us
whispering, whispering down resigned
to the state of things, to itself:
to America, Bly and to quiet.

II

In the black hall of the building
crash of boards dropped, pools of melting snow
and lights here and there from passageways.
Hammers. The janitor being talked to upstairs.
We move through the rooms, jam
boards to hold doors tight, lock the big windows,
nail others shut,
slide out the classroom chairs to be
piled one by one against entrances,
tighten wire across wood that could move
to let in the day. But into the flickering noise:
doubts.

"This place is a sieve, we'll never hold it."
"If the police come now or come early
  this handful of us is lost for nothing."
  And is this where your life changes, your job goes
  to another town, the spectre of clubs and gas,
  shoving helmets and jail?
  The building slows; some faces drift in the hall:
"The place is a sieve, we'll never hold it."
"If we had three hundred instead of thirty, we could. . . ."
"Let's just leave the blockades and go."
  Some others go past in the darkness, carrying
  a heavy plank.

  Again in the open air, I want to learn
  depths of commitment or cowardice
  crossing the empty streets with some others
  to the cold car. What does this leaving mean?
  Black flashes of levering a huge partition
  against some windows, slumping to a chair, considering
  where does your life change, if not here. Maybe
  nothing will happen. What then, but to have learned
  what you would do or not do? Footsteps
  on the snowy sidewalks leading into the building.
  Footsteps out on the ice in the early, early morning.

III

So of all of us who began, fifteen are in custody by noon.
And Bly in the afternoon speaks softly
of a great despair in the land: like the deep snow
out of the lounge windows where he talks, easing down
on the hills and frozen trees. Only fifteen left and willing
to face the massed police and be busted, and Bly
speaks of them slowly, waving his red wristband of support
for the Milwaukee Fourteen, who napalmed draft records
months ago on cement in the sunshine. Bly in the evening
sighs as a wind, his sweet voice soothing
and crackling like a gentle fire in a grate somewhere
warm against a cold night, saying how much
America longs to sleep, longs to forget its Empire
and the wars of Empire, the hatred of all the men of the world
it can burn but not own. Sleep! Bly cries. Sleep!
And in jail, the others say later, it was too cold
to sleep, but I nod in the back of the theatre
mumbling yes, yes
I would love sleep, an end to this testing myself
and my words against plans, against actions, afraid
in movements and struggle where love and trust
are not born yet, too new, too beaten by fear,
guilt, doubt. Sleep, and an end to optimism
trying to cheer myself and perhaps another
with the anecdotes of history: with a certainty and
joy that escaped me, it seems,
in this past night when the bitter bone
of a sure defeat seemed worthless
compared to running away to the daily reverses of
talk. Bly, the winter, and slumber swirl in as a fog
of despair at myself, my retreat from myself.
Where am I now in Colorado?
There is so much snow.

Tom Wayman

Casual Labor

Up on the scaffold at the brick face:
money.
High over the floor, with acid-pail and wire brush:
cleaning money.
Bits of plaster and old grime
are worked off the bricks.
The dollars come clean.

They appear as little rippling flags
that gleam like coins.
A forest of paper strips
that glitter and sparkle in a field.
They are in the brick. In the clock.
In the heavy lumber.

Sometimes for a moment the money goes.
The weight of a board
can push out the mind.
Or when each breath is free of planks.

Mostly, though, there is money. Nothing
for the money to buy.
Only the crisp crowd of bills
fluttering, in a casual union.

Tom Wayman

Loneliness of the Unemployed

One morning I wake up and my manhood is gone.
I cannot believe it. Then, faintly
I hear it crying. Thin, muffled peeps
from the eyeless mouth. I tear out of bed
and begin to search,
turning over books and clothes.
After a frantic minute, I discover the thing
alone in my billfold on a chair.

It is lonely without the body.
I look at the hands and they do not say anything.
They cannot tell me what they are for.
Also the feet. The chest and stomach
can breathe and be hungry
but neither can say a word.
Food is embarassed. Rice on my fork
looks the other way when it is brought to my mouth.

Once I woke in the night
and heard the body talking.
It spoke of its shame. It told itself
it was going away.
I broke in, to try to explain.
Silence.
We rolled back to back and pretended to sleep.

I stop a man on the street and begin to discuss myself.
He interrupts to assure me my situation is not my fault.
"But when you are poor you should not be in love,
have children, enjoy yourself," he tells me.
"These things are for people with money."
I want to thank him
but he has begun an argument with his newspaper.
The printer's ink is quite abusive,
wrangling and hooting over a detail.

Once I had a trade as a writer
but I left because I did not want to lie.
I became a teacher, and taught lies.
At last I just talked, but the language
knew I was lying. The words
ran out of my mouth and told everyone
what a fraud I am.
It is lonely without even words.
There are no women without money.
But even without money, I do not want to stop being a man.
I cannot even stop being lonely.

Tom Wayman

*Statement

Everywhere I have lived I have watched and been part of a
people trying to live out their lives against a particular economic
and social system. I say that we live "against" this system,
because by and large it does not make life easy for anybody.
Nor does it seem very good for the land of this continent.
And it is the conflict between ourselves and our form of social
organization that lies behind, around, under and throughout
my poems.

The difficulty in my writing has always been to express the conflict
in a way that doesn't seem preachy, rhetorical, windy. I have
not found it easy to write about our own moment in history and
the troubles we find in it.

I think poetry is finally about freedom. Not just about the glorious
events of our struggle toward a better life, but around the free-
dom that is a man looking at a tree, or at the ocean, or at a meal.
Or at himself. There was a time when I thought as Bertolt
Brecht writes in his poem *To Posterity*: that those who wish to
lay the foundations of kindness by battling the system cannot
themselves afford to be kind. Now it seems to me that unless those
fighting for kindness are themselves kind, they will never know
what kindness is even if they achieve it.

So now my poems want to go off and find what is good in this life.
Now my poems want to be exactly as gentle as human flesh
and bone.

Ian Young

Sky/Eyes

On Earth,
as I rested my fingers on your hands,
how often my eyes would look into yours,
and how much we could tell
from the colours of eyes:
Brown eyes are solid, unbluffable,
strong and unchanging . . .
Dark blue eyes look forward,
to words and action spilled in a moment . . .
Green eyes like mine are cautious, intuitive,
like a cat's and slightly sinister . . .
Grey eyes are sad –
quiet, and strangely appealing.
Then, there are those light blue eyes –
Adriatic or Arctic – clear and cool,
honest, and infinitely gentle;
eyes of the child, the innocent,
open to the ideal, and the winter:
Rimbaud's eyes, and Lawrence's . . .
Looking into them,
you could see the sky,
cloudless, fresh and bright.
Your eyes were like that . . .
Here,
it is so quiet
as I fly.

Ian Young

*Statement

My primary reason for writing is to bring into consciousness,
to establish connections, and so to gain more control of my reality,
and to help whoever reads my work to gain more control of his.

When someone tells me a poem of mine has brought something
into focus or shown him some quality or meaning that he *almost*
knew but couldn't quite 'grasp' or 'put his finger on' before,
I know the poem has been successful for him, that through the
poem he has become more 'in touch' with himself and his world.

Dale Zieroth

The Hunters of the Deer

The ten men will dress in white
to match the snow and leave the last
farmhouse and the last woman, going
north into the country of the deer. It
is from there, and from past there, that
the wind begins that can shake
every window in the house and leaves
the woman wishing she had moved away
five years and five children ago.

During the day the father of her children
will kill from a distance. With the others
he will track and drive each bush
and at least once he will kill before
they stop and come together for
coffee in scratched quart jars. And
sometimes the November sun will glint
on the rifles propped together in the snow.

In the evening, as they skin and gut,
they talk about the one that ran three
miles on a broken leg and the bitch wolf
they should have shot and how John
the bachelor likes eating more than
hunting and they pass the whiskey
around to keep warm. In the house
the woman makes a meal from pork.

These men are hunters and later,
standing in bright electrically lighted
rooms they are sometimes embarassed with the
blood on their clothes and although the
woman nods and seems to understand,
she grows restless with their talk.
She has not heard another woman in fourteen days.

And when they leave, the man sleeps
and his children sleep while the woman
waits and listens for the howling of
wolves. And to the north, the grey
she-wolf smells the red snow and howls.
She also is a hunter of the deer.
Tonight, while other hunters sleep, she
drinks at the throat.

Dale Zieroth

Father

Twice he took me in his hands and shook
me like a sheaf of wheat, like a dog shakes
a snake, as if he meant to knock out my tongue
and grind it under his heel right there
on the kitchen floor. I never remembered
what he said or the warnings he gave; she
always told me afterwards, when he
had left and I had stopped my crying. I
was eleven that year and for seven more years
I watched his friends laughing and him
with his great hands rising and falling
with every laugh, smashing down on his knees
and making the noise of a tree when it cracks
in winter. Together they drank chokecherry
wine and talked of dead friends and the
old times when they were young and because
I never thought of getting old, their
youth was the first I knew of dying.

Sunday before church he would trim
his fingernails with the hunting knife
his East German cousins had sent, the same
knife he used for castrating pigs and
skinning deer: things that had nothing
to do with Sunday. Communion once
a month, a shave every third day, a
good chew of snuff, these were the things
that helped a man to stand in the sun for
eight hours a day, to sweat through each
cold hail storm without a word, to freeze
fingers and feet to cut winter wood, to do
the work that bent his back a little more
each day down toward the ground.

Last Christmas, for the first time, he
gave presents, unwrapped and bought
with pension money. He drinks mostly coffee
now, sleeping late and shaving everyday.
Even the hands have changed: white, soft,
unused hands. Still he seems content
to be this old, to be sleeping in the middle
of the afternoon with his mouth open as if there
is no further need for secrets, as if he is
no longer afraid to call his children "Fools!"
for finding different answers, different lives.

Dale Zieroth

Poem for a year ago, on
the death of Pierre Laporte

A year ago, we boarded the bus for Montreal,
left behind the downtown apartment
and felt safe. We sat across the aisle from each other
till Kingston. From then on it rained
and we talked of things that matched
the night and the colourless blur of lights.
Around us passengers smoked or hushed children
and everyone except the driver and those
who sat beside strangers made plans for sleep.

That night the students rioted while we
watched television, refusing to go over again
the arguments on revolution and oppression,
minority rights and the FLQ. Our plan had been
to leave these behind in the downtown apartment,
if not there, then somewhere on the bus. There
was no preparation for the sound from the street
that left us naked in our clothes, that left no space
for different sounds coming out of the past: the nights
of driving fast over loose gravel roads somewhere
in the back country where cops can't find you,
your belly tight with beer, your ears ringing
with the noise of a couple struggling
in the backseat. And the music, at full volume,
telling you to be young or wild or both.

Our journeys have become shorter, away
from cities, up towards Land's End or Christian Island
where the big newspapers are sometimes a day late.
Here we can forget those grand plans we made
from small safe places a year ago, before
we ran and thought by running
to escape. Now we want to freeze everything.
The bird in flight. The touching of hands.
The sniper's bullet before it breaks
the warm reluctant skin. . . .

Dale Zieroth

Across Canada, West from Toronto

Before Winnipeg, only the familar well-travelled
road, weaving in and out of the ageless
evergreen bush . . .

Across the top of Saskatchewan we ate
Sweet Marie chocolate bars and counted
everything that moved: the new birds, the
hitchhikers, gophers. We formed alliances
with the car ahead and the car behind,
travelling this way for fifty miles, like
partners in a dance. Ahead of us, a country
forever too large for one man's mind; behind us,
more of the same.

Edmonton looked like Winnipeg, and
Winnipeg had looked like something else . . .

Moving west, the world rises and the horizon
peaks, a mile above the timberline. We roar
through rock cuts between valleys, across valleys
filled with mist and swollen rivers, places
pioneers never went or went at twenty miles a day.
Split Peak, Wild Horse Lake, Glacier: names
for the untamed and places enough to convince you
these mountains will never change, that of all things
they have come the closest to lasting forever.

There is always as much road ahead as
there is behind: this is a fact of continents.
We stop for a moment, beside this road
the length of the country, to check our maps,
and then move on, dreaming of the Pacific.

Dale Zieroth

*Statement

Two years ago I decided to leave the prairies and come to Toronto.
It was an uneasy decision. The prairies, though at times oppres-
sive, had the safety of familiarity. And there was always plenty
of room.

When I arrived in Toronto I spent the first year in a ten dollar
a week room on St. Clair Avenue, miserable, lonely and wishing
I'd never come. I turned out poem after poem, none of them
very good. I tried going back to Manitoba, but found that whatever
niche I once had there no longer existed. Gradually, I adopted
Toronto as home base. The prairies ceased to exist as the singular
retreat from the ills of city life and I was able to write about
them objectively, as a witness. The result was a series of poems
about hunters, school houses, towns, journeys.

Meanwhile I discovered the city and became involved in the
free school movement, part of the counter-culture. Inside six
months I had dropped out, exhausted and dissatisfied. This failure
to become part of a culture of one's choice, like the unsuccessful
attempts to return to the culture of the prairies, not only became a
major concern, but gave a new perspective from which to
write. The result seems to be that I am working toward a poetry
where the objective fact is king, facts like hunters, subways,
traffic, riots. Hopefully it is a poetry where each poem is like an
essay, representing not one moment but many, based on
what is familiar to most urban Canadians but seldom comfortable
or safe.